THE Pugilist's DAUGHTER

POEMS

Judith Lynn Antelman

The Pugilist's Daughter
Copyright © 2022 Judith Lynn Antelman
Cover Art: Todd Windley, Designer
Author Photo: Luis Vieira

All rights reserved. Blue Jade Press, LLC, retains the right to reprint this book. Permission to reprint poems from this collection must be obtained by the author.

ISBN 978-1-7374758-2-8
Library of Congress Control Number: 2022934909

Published by:

Blue Jade Press, LLC

Blue Jade Press, LLC
Vineland, NJ 08360
www.bluejadepress.com

for Mama, with love

And dreams are faces with large eyes and weak chins and broad brows that get smashed by the fists of square faces.

–Jean Toomer

CONTENTS

LEAVING HOME

Phone Call – January 16, 2020	1
A Sort of Beginning	2
Still Life With Cars—A User's Guide	3
When My Sister and I Were Little Kids	6
The Pugilist's Wife	8
The Punch	10
The Pugilist in Twelve Rounds	12
Love Means Nothing	15
Run Little Girl, Run	17
Piano Lessons, A Refuge	18

WITH. ABANDON

Boston	23
Trains Are a Failed Romance	24
Hunger	26
Assumptions	28
Phone Call – February 13, 2020	30
What Else Is There	31
Collision	32
After the One That Broke Me	34
The No of Us	37
Carrot Cake at the Altar	38

ODYSSEY, LOST

Kraków Square	45
Hollow (While Thinking About Primo Levi)	46
Nocturne	48
Is That Himmler Biting His Hind Paw	51
In the Warsaw Ghetto, April 1941	53
Phone Call – March 11, 2020	55
Bosnia Update, May 1992	56

Bread Line	57
Roses of Sarajevo	58
To Be Continued	60
Riven	61

TOMBS: WHILE A CITY SLEEPS

Hold On, Manhattan, Hold On	67
Beyond Wonderland	69
David, Where Are You Now?	71
Because My Country Broke	73
Breath	75
Shall We Dance	76
Phone Call – September 23, 2020	78

WHAT IS HOME

When There Are Nine	83
Revisiting Brooklyn	85
We'll Build and We'll Fight	87
Memory, In Five Parts	90
Las Vegas	94
Canyon Ballad	96
Heat	98
Funeral	101
The Pugilist's Daughter	103
Phone Call – November 29, 2020	105

Notes	107
Acknowledgements	110

LEAVING HOME

Oh, but to be a boxer not a poet,

—Wisława Szymborska

PHONE CALL – JANUARY 16, 2020

6:30 p.m. in New Jersey   it's 3:30 p.m. in Las Vegas
i'm on a daily phone call with Mama   i like Vegas
she says   i have nice friends   one of them   her
family lives in New Yawk   i like that   i like when
people here   ask me   where are you from   i say
New Yawk   they say   who lives in   New Yawk
who i tell them   bright people   live in New Yawk
bright people   don't ask me again   she asks me
how do they not know bright people   in New Yawk
she laughs   i'm taking a walk   they're not bright
people probably right i know   i know   i'm repeating
myself i'm repeating i know   i know   i'll walk now

how does she know   i wonder   a walk? i wonder

A SORT OF BEGINNING

my father	is not	my story
a boxer	never	a poet
an engineer	always	a writer
a painter	maybe	a pianist
a dancer	one day	a runner
between a line	our	verbal sparring
inside a ring	hope	sustained our friction
on the ropes	until	the day my father died

        this is our story

STILL LIFE WITH CARS—A USER'S GUIDE

Stuck in the Holland Tunnel. After midnight. Christmas Eve. Squeezed into the backseat of my father's Jell-O red '67 Mustang. Sometime in the seventies. Wedged in the middle hump seat between my two sisters. Mom and Dad in front bucket seats. Last night of Chanukah. We lit menorah candles at my grandparent's house in Flatbush-Midwood. My older sister stood too close. My father doused her hair the way I watch him drench his car. Eleven family members gathered around five menorahs. Later my father would say he was the only genius armed with a spray bottle.

> my father was an engineer
> he loved to break things
> or take them apart and then fix
>
> everything, especially cars,
> tennis racquets, family—
> my father was a fixer

My mother tells my father to take the Lincoln Tunnel. Less traffic. He insists on the Holland Tunnel because it's quicker from Brooklyn to Passaic. Logical and wastes less gas. My father always lectured about logic and the price of gas. I wanted to get home fast to read my new books that Grandma Rose gave me for Chanukah. I get dizzy reading in cars. Especially crammed into my father's tiny matchbox car. I tried to tune out my parents. They fought about everything. No, they didn't fight. My father yelled. My mother listened. My father threw tantrums. My mother caught them.

> you can fix cars but you cannot fix
> sadness and you cannot fix people—
> especially sad mothers—nothing fixes
>
> sadness but i did not know this on
> Christmas Eve and the last night
> of Chanukah stuck in the Holland Tunnel

Hundreds of cars. Jammed into one lane. Probably an accident. Even if I could see, our windows are shut tight to prevent us from contracting carbon monoxide poisoning. My father drew diagrams about how open windows in tunnels would kill us. And then, three nuns dressed like Julie Andrews in *The Sound of Music* appear in the shut-down lane. Three nuns. Dancing the worried dance. Like when they sang, "How Will We Solve a Problem Like Maria." They were jumping up and down, arms flailing to attract attention. This was before cell phones. Their car was broken. Nobody stopped. Except my father. I knew he would help the nuns. The same way I knew my mother would resent him for fixing another strangers' car.

> i don't know if he ever tried but i know
> he never fixed her sadness—he fixed a pool
> table in our living room, a ping-pong table
>
> in the den, a boxing ring in our basement,
> a train set on the dining room table—
> year after year, she watched him fix things

I scream out like a Jack Russell. I had seen *The Sound of Music* at least five times but I didn't know nuns were allowed to drive. They were always singing and dancing in Salzburg. My father disappears under the hood of their car. I jump out of our Mustang to dance with them. Or just stand next to them. I was too excited to remember about carbon monoxide poisoning and he couldn't see me. Soon I'd be dead and look like the kids my father drew in the diagrams.

> my mother stares out the car window the way
> she stares when my father surprises her
> on Saturdays with five tennis friends and she
>
> cooks breakfast for them and he leaves again
> to play more tennis—she keeps flipping
> pancakes and omelets standing at the stove   staring

I am standing in that toxic tunnel. Happy. With three dancing nuns. Their broken car. A Chanukah miracle. I pray to stay in that filthy tunnel forever. I pretend they are my parents. So I don't have to go home with my real parents—with my mother who was always sad and my father who only knew how to break and fix things. But did not know how to fix her sadness.

> i dream i live in a monastery with nuns
> and we sing and dance and nobody ever
> yells or breaks things and my mother
>
> lives there and my father stays home
> and collects broken cars in our driveway
> and everybody lives happily—

Three weeks after Chanukah, a 36-square-inch box of chocolate arrives at our doorstep with a note that reads, "Dear Mr. A, You are a true Christmas miracle. Bless you and your family." Inside this box are 50 individually wrapped mini chocolates—a real Christmas miracle. Only one of numerous thank you gifts my father received with every repaired carburetor, transmission, brake—

> it makes me sad i believed
> marrying off Maria
> would fix everything

WHEN MY SISTER AND I WERE LITTLE KIDS

we once removed all the lids from the tiny glass
jars in our father's basement workshop—his sacred

shrine of tools forbidden to our touch—we swapped
lids and jars confusing hundreds of washers and screws

bolts and nails—metals he would use to build our
bookcases and take-apart cars—metals he would meld

to quell his moods—brass and nickel and bronze tumbled
like confetti onto tiles and grout—it was the day our father

promised us Rutt's Hut hot dogs and Holstein's ice cream
but stayed out too long at the tennis courts perfecting

his serve—we were bored so we passed time
rearranging his shrine and then my sister grabbed a mop

and bucket of water to wash the basement floor—penance
before punishment—puddles formed and swirled across

linoleum and when our father came home from tennis
he slid on his ass and slit his right thumb on four

two-inch nails—frozen on the watery basement floor
in rare silence his eyes fix upon my little sister—he stands

still   silent   Dunlop racquet in his hand stretching
reaching overhead—we watch from an old brown couch

across the room   he steps back   sets up his perfect
serve but first a voice cries out   SHUT UP—my little sister

a few years on this earth screams at him—he stands
nine feet away from us and smashes every glass jar

with his textbook topspin and allows her
a pass—broken glass kayaks between confusion

and a perfect serve as he inches toward
my sister and me—CLEAN UP THIS MESS

we were eight and four

THE PUGILIST'S WIFE

This one's the hardest—so I buried it
with my third-grade plastic cat-eye
frames and orange-purple bellbottoms
There she was my Mama—

with my third-grade plastic cat-eyes
in the boxing ring   beside him
There she was my Mama—
taking hits   avoiding corners

in the boxing ring   beside him
She hid the scars inside her apple Bundt cake
taking hits   avoiding corners
There she was my Mama—ducking his thrown leftovers

She hid the scars inside her apple Bundt cake
stayed up late with me writing nightmares
There she was my Mama—ducking his thrown leftovers
dodging jars of PB&J he smashed against the kitchen nook

stayed up late with me writing nightmares
There she was my Mama—never a cleaner, always a cook
dodging glass jars of honey he smashed against the kitchen nook
This one's the hardest—I denied it   could not write it

There she was my Mama—never a cleaner, always a cook
A sustained right hook flung her fifty years later to memory care
This one's the hardest—I denied it   could not write it
I buried it with my father's fists in my mother's shame

A sustained right hook flung her fifty years later to memory care
This one's the hardest—so I buried it with my younger self
I buried it with my father's fists in my mother's shame
Here she is my Mama   her cauliflowered brain   her boxer's brain

This one's the hardest—so I buried it with my younger self
and orange-purple bellbottoms
Here she is my Mama   her cauliflowered brain   her boxer's brain
This one's the hardest—so I buried it

THE PUNCH

I can't forget that night.
The night I learned I don't want kids.
The night I learned lonely is safer.
The night his fist broke through their bedroom wall.

The night I learned I don't want kids.
The night I inked Mom's black and blues into my journal.
The night his fist broke through their bedroom wall.
I want to forget that night.

The night I inked Mom's black and blues into my journal.
I can't forget Dad's screams.
I want to forget that night.
I sat on my closet floor listening to Dad throw jars.

I can't forget Dad's screams.
I tasted fear the way eight-year-olds tasted ice cream.
I sat on my closet floor listening to Dad throw jars.
I hid under my bed and wished Dad dead.

I tasted fear the way eight-year-olds tasted ice cream.
I remember Mom's eyes after, thick with dread.
I hid under my bed and wished Dad dead.
I can't forget Mom's pleas.

I remember Mom's eyes after, thick with dread.
I'm tired of trying to expunge that night.
I can't forget Mom's pleas.
My hands armed with boxing gloves.

I'm tired of trying to expunge that night.
When I started writing inside my bedroom closet.
My hands armed with boxing gloves.
I'm sick of memory's holding pattern.

When I started writing inside my bedroom closet.
The night I learned lonely is safer.
I'm sick of memory's holding pattern.
I can't forget that night.

THE PUGILIST IN TWELVE ROUNDS

To love my father is to love his wounds.
            —Cathy Linh Che

At the crossroads of strained speech
and another breath, the boxer shoves
tomorrow like a scalpel in his heart.
His days fall flat and futile like a
knockout on a canvas and the boxer's

purple scabs and scars and bruiser
broken vows are drenched inside
a vat of Jack and Jim and Johnnie.
When he was 18, the Golden Gloves
middleweight once split open a man's

jaw with an upper cut at the final bell.
After the match, he sauntered home
to Broadway and 181st Street, inhaled
a Bud and burger, lay down in the dark
face up flat on the kitchen floor

and played Chopin on a Victrola. The pugilist
was my father and a boxer and I sensed
the difference at eight-years-old when
he taught me to play tennis and chess.
He chided me for my Queen's Pawn opening

and wonky backhand while he drove us across
the Hudson to the Hologram Museum
and Chinatown Ice-Cream Factory—a bittersweet
chocolate-lychee-ice-cream memory of New York City
Sunday sacrament with the pugilist—a frequent stain

beneath my skin the strongest bleach did not remove.
In a Hackensack hospital room, I will never
smell again, the pugilist starts to die. Surgery
sacrificed his legs and speech. Mugged his
punch and serve. All he knew was vanquished.

This is knockout. Stolen, a familiar bellowing
of childhood—my daily alarm clock. Tonight,
the boxer's former shrill is a shadow's whisper.
Staring down from a precipice of regret and pride,
the boxer's grit reached his limits of muscle memory.

When I was eight years old, my father taught me
how to box and I have been sparring my way
into and out of his corners ever since. In one
of the hundreds of boxing articles he imposed
on my memory, I once read boxing was like math,

calculating angles. I was destined to fail his beloved
Geometry because I had it all backwards, he said.
I believed in metaphor and meter the way a boxer
believes in footwork and timing. Boxing, angles, tennis
dodged my southpaw. Forty-Love. The pugilist

is winning. I don't know how to break his serve.
This is shadow boxing. I wait for a sign he would steal
another breath, recall his favorite knockouts—
Louis vs. Schmeling, Marciano vs. Walcott, Ali vs. Frazier.
He freezes time and turns back clocks to 1949.

Hearing a solitary boxer is on par
with an ocean's circular rise and fall
rise and fall of the pugilist and his daughter
reconciling a history of oblique prisms,
open wounds. Inside a hospital room,

he stares through me. "Where was I?"
A thin alien voice. Strained words.
 In boxing and tennis, timing is everything.
"Where was I?" A slow smile. Apologies.

LOVE MEANS NOTHING

      I am lying near my bedroom window
All I hear is snow falling   My father

wakes me at 6AM with his winning backhand
and topspin   Serves to me my handmade

pink and purple piggybank   A gift
from Grandma Rose and Grandpa Harry

Sitting at my bedroom window   All I hear
is snow falling   Ceramic shards

shatter against four hot-pink
flower-painted bedroom walls

All I hear is snow
Falling   Pink and purple

pottery debris skip across
my upper lip and left arm

      Gazing out a classroom window
Fourth grade   All I hear is

Snow falling   I daydream away
science and math   Long division

Andrew and Geoffrey lead
the class   Photosynthesis

I sneak a peek at John Z
my kindergarten crush

Dream we run away
from school　　　away

from home　away　away　away　All
　　　　　　　　　　I hear is snow falling

Henrietta scolds me for daydreaming
away chlorophyll and fractions

Ivy sneak-eats candy bars and offers me
Bit-O-Honey, PEZ, and Good & Plenty

　　　After school　　standing on
the playground　　waiting

　　　　　　for my father　a Honda motorcycle
　　　　　　revs across the street　All I hear is

Snow
falling　　Jump on he shouts　　grab

your helmet　tilt right　hold on tight
or the wind'll knock you out　　I am

sitting at my bedroom window　I don't
know how to blame or tame him

so I chisel future　out of shards and dreams and snow
　　　　　　　　　　　　　　　falling
　　　and remember when he told me
　　　　　　　　in tennis love means having zero

RUN LITTLE GIRL, RUN

Away from Dad who tossed clothes
like tennis balls out bedroom windows
and from Mom whose eyes were

puffy as my pillows—pleading with her
husband to stop smashing glass and hurling
objects just because he lost a tennis match

I had to run from family car trips, Dad screaming
while tailgating every car, middle finger up—Mom
clenching her knees with fists full of fear. I had to run

toward Sunday drives I only read about where
siblings sing in open air *the hills are alive*...windows
down breezy *with the sound of music* laughing, easy

I had to run from childhood bedroom walls
that absorbed a shrieking dad and witnessed school
permission slips torn to shreds and brawls

that hollered—why didn't you clean up? I did,
I barely heard my mother whisper. His infamous
backhand followed by a splat. I feared she'd be

dead at the end of those so I had to run to erase
seventeen years of phones torn from walls, sounds of
shattered lamps crashing inside

                pretending family   pretending home

When Mom and Dad danced at weddings, ballroom
floors cleared, cameras flashed, applause boomed
        How happy they appeared   so I ran toward

PIANO LESSONS, A REFUGE

Moody Beethoven sonatas and nocturnes by Chopin.
A cold, damp studio on the second floor.
Tremulous fingers, unsteady hands

Stumble on a keyboard, a foreign land.
I trip over sixteenth notes from intricate scores.
Moody Beethoven sonatas and nocturnes by Chopin.

Mrs. M's melancholy. Strict drill commands.
Beethoven's *Pathétique in C minor.*
Tremulous fingers, unsteady hands

Practice for hours on Mrs. M's Steinway Concert Grand.
She fled Russia's Jewish bans with dreams to perform
Moody Beethoven sonatas and nocturnes by Chopin.

Instead she started a school. Armed with a metronome.
Softened by a silver mane that framed years of despair.
Tremulous fingers, unsteady hands—

Reminders of Mrs. M's helpful demands.
Lento, sotto voce. *Nocturne in C-sharp minor.*
Moody Beethoven sonatas and nocturnes by Chopin.
Tremulous fingers, unsteady hands.

WITH. ABANDON.

Loneliness is solitude with a problem.

–Maggie Nelson

BOSTON

We learn myths about love at age three.
A stranger on the T wearing Red Sox attire
And a tuxedo jacket smiles at me

In my Levi's jeans and long-sleeve T
That reads Save Darfur.
We learn myths about love at age three.

Will stranger attend a baseball game or symphony?
Will he invite me I wonder, as I recall last October
Your tuxedo jacket smiles at me

When you cook blueberry pancakes, brew Colombian coffee
But do not invite me to the opera and I pretend not to care.
We learn myths about love at age three.

After breakfast, I seek clues I'm your Persephone.
Between oceans and suns you'd fight for me like a Centaur.
Your tuxedo jacket smiles at me.

Memories inhabit a North End café consuming ouzo and cannoli.
No Pegasus rescue, your ghost sits beside me in an empty chair.
We learn myths about love at age three.
A tuxedo jacket smiles at me.

TRAINS ARE A FAILED ROMANCE

        I used to believe love was a train flying
at a speed I did not know how to sustain
           could not sustain   December 5PM
          icicles oscillate like raindrops

        chandeliers   threaten
suspend evening plans
       newsflash:
            resident halts rush hour

        sometimes I want to forget   not all
just the night I believed everything
          was possible in a crystal-cut December sky
              my father pointed to a full moon

        look look look at the man in the moon
I asked him why is the moon
       a man and not a woman
           men are smarter he said

        I was ten years old and stopped believing
in fairy tales and nursery rhymes
        I stopped believing in opaque answers
            stuck and squeezed and squirming

       deep inside a bell jar
I stopped believing in the moon
        instead I believed in dolphins
            magnolia ice fog cerulean blue—

                    sometimes I want to stand on an ocean
in the middle   feel vibrations of an oncoming wave
            gushing surging surf   hands at my side
                        tempting chance   waiting   waiting   waiting

            I stop hearing noise
I hear only distance   silence
            whitecaps dance skyward around my belly
                        waiting on a wave

            waves are failed romance
I used to believe romance
            was an ocean swelling at a speed
                        I did not know how

            to sustain   could not sustain
a sun sets over a sea of speculation
            waiting on a wave   waiting
                        on failed romance

            newsflash: young girl
wants to swim *like dolphins can swim*
            drowns in the middle of an ocean—
                        sometimes I want to stand still

HUNGER

I spend an entire year speaking to his palms
        and veiny forearms because his eyes frighten
me. I fear the sapphire in his irises will sever

my lips and tongue. I inject nursery rhymes
into his sonnets as an excuse for another
        Friday revision with his limbs. I count

the hours until we meet at 3PM and I know
        it must end. Desire is the distance between
goodbye and hello. I sit alone on a park bench

in Sheep Meadow and watch a woman breastfeed
her baby while a man rubs her abdomen. Plump
        blue snowflakes descend onto the woman's breast

The man removes her blouse. I am sitting in McSorley's
        next to my poet laureate. Patience is also
a form of action, wrote Rodin.

I stare at his veiny forearms.
He downs a pint. Outside it is snowing
        in September. Inside a woman's diamond

wedding ring tumbles from a pocket, twirls
        around a sawdust-covered floor. I ignore
a marriage between glint and wood chips

Fantasy is remaining inside a myth
because real does not fit.
        I walk home alone toward Central Park.

I sit on a bench and stare at three figures
        huddled on a lawn like a Rodin
in a silent empty Sheep Meadow.

Plump blue snowflakes
mask a woman's milky naked flesh
                              Insatiably, two figures eat

ASSUMPTIONS

Eggs are always safe to order in a diner
people always say that—
people in New Jersey

What about salmonella, I wonder,
or raw eggs or bloody yolks
or crazy chickens

I don't want to understand suicide

This morning at Tic Toc Diner,
I heard a fully tattooed 30-something
girl tell her girlfriend,

my parent's vow renewal party is tonight
and I don't want to go it's all the way in Brooklyn
but if I skip it I'll jump off the Bayonne Bridge

Do couples renew vows to prevent divorce or suicide?

I wanted to ask her why Bayonne
and not the more romantic Brooklyn Bridge
She wants to die in Jersey

More romantic—the diner state. I read online
New Jersey has the lowest suicide rate in the US
she may want to skew the data

I didn't want to know her name

She ordered fried eggs and Buffalo wings. I hope
she goes to the vow renewal party. I know couples
in desperate need of vow renewal parties

Stuck in Locked out Trapped above Forced under
I watch them amputate their dreams
as they fly their kids to the Ivy League

They eschew diners and fried eggs

Bayonne told her girlfriend
her wings and eggs tasted so crappy
she wanted to die

She should have ordered
Rye toast. Another safe
Jersey diner food

Then I noticed on her left forearm
an eggshell blue tattoo of two baby chicks
that looked like Easter Peeps

I want to die she said

All I wanted to do was cook fried eggs
and Buffalo wings and feed her while
driving to the vow renewal party together

Sometimes I understand why people commit suicide

They are mis-under-water   They cannot
They do not   They are drowning
Bayonne walked out of Tic Toc Diner alone

Her girlfriend continued eating crappy fried eggs
and Buffalo wings on her own. She ordered
triple layer chocolate ganache cake and laughed

She looked relieved.   I assumed.

PHONE CALL – FEBRUARY 13, 2020

it's pitch black outside   Mama says   it's too dark
i tell her it's night time   do you see any stars i ask
she laughs   and says   at this part   of the night
i can't tell   a star from   an umbrella   from an eagle
i ask   how about clouds   do you see any clouds
she laughs at this part   of the night   i don't know
a cloud   from a balloon   are you happy Mama
are you happy she asks   yes i lie   she asks again
are you really happy   or do you say yes for my sake

i miss you so much i want to say   i'm happy Mama

WHAT ELSE IS THERE

On MLK day in a Unitarian church
I'm steeped in sunshine speeches skepticism
I listen to a pastor preaching

like a beloved Buddhist warrior. Her
molasses muscular voice blends
purpose with pain, devotion with discipline

liability with love. I listen and scribble
the pastor's words into my program—
pain   discipline   love.

Is pain watching snow rise
outside a window   alone?
Does discipline diminish desire?

When does love replace liability?
When a crowded sanctuary fills with voices singing
we'll walk hand in hand...we shall overcome?

Or during a 12-hour conversation at a café
in Berlin with a stranger I never see again?
I seek answers that do not apply

because I ask the wrong questions.
On MLK day I sit in a Unitarian church.
I sing. I stand. I hold a stranger's hand.

I seek refuge where lost and comfort collide
because lonely   beseeches patience.
I seek love because   because   because

COLLISION

Wanting you so much,
I run around town wearing
silky summer dresses

in the middle of a chilling
winter willing you to love me.
I slip on icy sidewalks insecure

in strappy slip-on sandals,
stumble into front row seats
at your opera debut, feign

my love for Verdi's *Nabucco*.
After years of mistaking
desire with tears,

I remember Nabucco's
Fenena and find my grit.
Four acts later I persevere.

At sunset in December,
a pale memory of an opera
debut—my view

a shattered streetlamp
transforms winter light
outside my fourth-floor

window—shards
of flickering amethyst
slice through peony pink

and lupine blue
as I recall a failed
experiment—me and you.

Dusk when a kaleidoscope
of color weeps on slumbering
rooftops, a mango-berry

sorbet sky collapses
into melancholy. December
sunset crashes into lingerie

and Verdi's *Nabucco*. Needing
more than wanting, I toss
my silky summer dresses

and strappy slip-on sandals
into the spaces between
longing and leaving.

AFTER THE ONE THAT BROKE ME

     into a splintered glass mosaic
  I learned dancing alone in fear
is safer than dancing securely

in your resistant arms. With you,
  I shared moments in a day—
    my friend's daughter Annie

    is now Artie. I lost my job.
  I miss Bowie. I'm starting an MF
A—mid-syllable you pivot

Your fire-orange azaleas
  steal you away and I am
    cracked open. Split into

    the Milky Way and no *Starman*
waiting in the sky. I am sleep
walking into crumbs like

sentient seagulls in sand chasing
  scraps seeking stardust searching
    a starless sky awake alone afraid

    aware of a familiar song I seized
  when you would not dance with me
on Frenchman Street, stand beside

me when I needed you, read
  my poetry. In my fantasy
    I pull ten wooden beams

        from your trellis and watch
     your garden of eden tumble
crumble (be)humble the way

my poems Un(mattered)
    splattered shattered into
        saturated crumbs when

        you wiped pork fat from
    your kitchen table with my
final draft. A stranger

told me if I ignore my anger
    I will never learn my heart.
        I thought of Tolstoy's Anna K

        Then we should find some artificial
    inoculation against love, as with smallpox
he wrote. How can the same flesh

feed me love and hurt on the same
    rainy Tuesday afternoon. Tempt me
        toward a train track. I am tired.

        Inoculate me. In a Maine BnB
    outside our window an ocean
watches seagulls in a starless sky

searching swells for scraps. I ask
    for crumbs I beg for more
        I need a cure so I dance

        outside and hide beneath an ocean's
    beating heart. I drift ashore until
my wound is a scar that bleeds no more.

I am learning how to be
        with me again. How to I am. How to
                scan a sky for shooting stars.

                How to laugh alone dance alone
        to Bowie in my narrow galley
kitchen forgetting to remember

not to bump into all six-foot-four
        of you. Somewhere *there's a Starman*
                waiting in the sky while stars tremble

                              like a sutured human heart

THE NO OF US

The last time I walked in Auschwitz, I recalled
us strolling hand in hand even though I recite
Kaddish and you sing the blues of B. B. King

and Lady Day. The last time I walked in Auschwitz,
I glimpsed a San Francisco rooftop fourth of July
midnight, fireworks bursting giggly girls rehearsing

clever ways to say "we fled Spring Valley during
the great white flight" and I squeezed your hand
tighter than the last time and you dared me

to say one word and I willed you to speak at least
ten or two. The last time I walked in Auschwitz,
I mined the final time we talked about the thick color

of my blood and your skin in a North Beach café.
The hostess ignored us and you squeezed my hand
tighter than the last time as I fantasized vaporizing

her. A color coordinated couple sat at our
window table sipped café au lait and mapped out
their Sunday. The last time I walked in Auschwitz,

I scratched my Grandma's name into a big fat
tree trunk with a piece of barbed wire and dotted
the "i" in Rosie with a saffron dandelion so it looked

like the star she wore on Yom Kippur the year
she taught me about a boy named Emmett Till.

CARROT CAKE AT THE ALTAR
—in memory of Kristine

PART I – BC
DECEASED RETURN TO SENDER
inked on a birthday card envelope I mailed to a best friend

DECEASED RETURN TO SENDER
I read one hundred times   words I do not understand

DECEASED RETURN TO
a memory   a conversation started at Pont Vecchio

RETURN TO
our endless walks in East and West Berlin
along the Ku'damm and Brandenburg Gate
"I think I won't grow old, I won't be long
for this place," you said. Casually,

as if reporting rain on the western side
of the Wall or another train strike in Milan.
Confused, I laughed and asked,
"Where should we go for dinner?"

We lost our way on the eastern side
of the Berlin Wall and for a moment
we were cold war spies until *Verboten.*
Raus. Schnell. Guns. Guards. Above

our heads a soldier in brass shouting,
Off the grass. Away from the Wall.
We laughed, flirted our way past
guns   guards   *verboten.*

Our favorite beer hall after
many rounds, you proclaim,
"One day you'll be in my wedding,
no vanilla cake or white veil or lies

or champagne toasts, only Guinness
pints and carrot cake at my altar."
Bemused, I joined your masquerade
and we clinked our beer steins

with strangers. In German,
we toasted your future
wedding   your future
husband   you had yet to meet

PART II – AD
I now pronounce you
I do you say   I do he says
(your new Christian husband)
No   I do not do

I want to scream
Where is the Guinness?
Where is the carrot cake?
My best friend? After Berlin

you unearthed journeys into the flesh
detached from the matter you said
Strange new words   speaking in tongues
laying on hands   Christ your savior

Passion your need   your shame
In sacraments you cowered   praying
You became a stranger speaking
in ~~foreign~~ tongues. I stopped asking why.

The only trinity blood flesh   death
a torment inside your womb
Verdi's Requiem echoed from
your husband's room where

he expected 'His' arrival to speak
through you   save you   lying
prostrate in agony   rushed
to the ER too late. I never believed

your new testament could fill up
the old holes. He stole your mind
force-fed psalms   prayers
you did not trust   you were lost

"I think I won't grow old,
I won't be long for this place."
Confused, I drank Guinness,
ate carrot cake at the altar   alone

ODYSSEY, LOST

*I cannot remember a time when I did not love Budapest.
And today, I'm just looking for memories.*

–Agnes A.

KRAKÓW SQUARE

I return to Kraków after occupation, wars, genocide.
I meander a town square—a poet, a Jew, a traveler
induced by ancient wounds and sounds of Klezmer.

Under cathedral hill, I hear shrill trumpets blare
Groups of tourists swarm around old panis selling
poppies, homemade crepes, and smelly cheese.

What I know of this historic square—selections,
deportations, who would live, and who would die
drifted in with scents of paczki, pierogi, borscht, and beer.

I watch pageants of little girls boast flaxen curls
and church dresses that swirl. Flirting teenage boys
and girls hide their lust from priests and nuns.

In this backyard of empires, I recall a labyrinth
of anxious human luggage forced into a convoy
destined eastward. Obedient clergy scurry out

of market square. Sprint away from sounds
of choking baggage, silenced cries,
                                    the Kaddish.

And from every spire across the square, I hear
the tintinnabulation signaling Sunday mass
is done. If a nation cannot endure its history—

My country will remain what it is what it was,
drowning its past in saviors and sins,
occupiers and occupied, poets and Chopin.

HOLLOW (WHILE THINKING ABOUT PRIMO LEVI)

From my fourth-floor walkup
above the Vistula River   I watch
a snowstorm in October   I wait
Snowbanks like your absence

suffocate   Inside a battered
hallway entrance of my address
I search my tin can postbox
for love letters you forgot

to mail months ago   Across
oceans   countries   time zones
you light another Salem   love
another woman while I will

a pre-war ten-pound telephone
to ring at midnight   Deafening
silence occupies my two-room
flat   unsolicited   I notice snow

looks different here   Polish snow
October snow   I dream your nicotine
lips will splice us to the Vistula   Choking
memories of your skin on top of her skin

shifting   skimming   lifting   expecting
me to understand you loved her once
but now   her crazy frightens you
yet you abide and lie beside her manic

fits   this and an ocean   your alibi
When I ask for you   my voice
frightens me against history's
bloodstained silence   Tenacious

hunger surges around me   feeds
my veins through an invisible I.V.
Familiar window panes divine cold
from desire   You do not write or call

Outside snowdrops fall into a river's endless tide
           I contemplate a not-so-famous suicide

NOCTURNE

Every difficulty slurred over will be a ghost to disturb your repose later on.
                                        –Chopin

August. Poland. A few months into my research. A futile attempt to understand genocide. How easily and swiftly it happens side by side a local population drinking coffee and holy water. Still afraid to walk inside a camp. Concentration. Extermination. The difference was the approach. Extermination camps housed the gas chambers and ovens that quickly murdered thousands of bodies at the same time. Efficient. Concentration camps killed with slave labor, disease, a rifle butt to the head, a bayonet. Starvation. The usual.

>   i remember your voice in the dark
>   i don't like poetry you whispered—
>   you gave me purple dahlias, your favorite flower

>   i remember your voice in the dark
>   an opera bass rehearsing Mozart—
>   i don't like opera but i pretended

Red poppies dance in the distance. The iconic gate at Auschwitz: ARBEIT MACHT FREI. I walk inside the 'work makes you free' gate for the tenth time, or hundredth. I've lost count. I return with Bennie, a Holocaust survivor from Kraków. We met in San Francisco while I was interviewing survivors, partisans, and an occasional nazi. Bennie wanted his memoirs written. I write. He remembers. We are a team. We meet in Poland. I live in Kraków these days. I visit Auschwitz-Birkenau too much. And today, a hot August Friday, we're back at Bennie's former residence.

>   after Auschwitz, he says, coffee
>   tastes like vinegar mixed with ash—
>   pansies and peonies smell like urine and gas
>
>   fluttering red poppies—a reminder
>   of fiery flesh spiraling skyward
>   in scorching yellow wind

We walk a few miles up a dirt road leading to Birkenau. Almost all of his family—63 relatives, including his parents—quiver six feet under these vast killing fields. Acres and acres of dirt mud bread wine body blood pebbles weeds dried leaves grass—the largest Jewish cemetery in the world. Mountains of earth here, rows of perfectly symmetrical tombstones there. Crosses. Absent a Star of David. Rows and rows of monuments for the dead, the Catholic dead.

>   he sits on a tombstone,
>   his ass beside a cross
>   seething, he lights up
>
>   and sucks on a joint—
>   daisies and daffodils wilt—
>   plagued by history
>
>   red poppies thrive—like
>   swastikas baiting his memory
>   in still fetid wind

Enough for today, he says. We ride the train back. Kraków, where some of the world's greatest poets lived and wrote and fled. From the station, it is a short walk to Kazimierz, Kraków's Jewish quarter. Centuries-old synagogues and Jewish cemeteries—tombstones stacked vertically 10-15 deep. Closer to the former Jewish ghetto, I smell strong Polish coffee and honey milled wine—miód pitny—

drifting out from open doors and windows of the new cafés that line the ancient square.

Former site of transports. Sunflowers and red poppies adorn every café table. Freshly baked cinnamon-apple strudel, honey cakes, walnut cookies infuse the air. Summon us toward Café Ariel. Klezmer bands comprised of violins, clarinets, trumpets, accordions play "Sunrise, Sunset." Tourists sing. Couples dance.

      i think of you and wonder
      if you are waltzing with your
      new bride tonight—do purple

      dahlias drape her hair or red poppies—
      Bennie lights up a joint—dances—
      sips a cup of Polish coffee

IS THAT HIMMLER BITING HIS HIND PAW?

Inside Poland's fragile borders, I seek out
a city I love. Kraków is a pungent memory.

Thirteenth-century cobblestones.
Sixteenth-century synagogues.

A discovery, an obsession. Swastikas
shoved sideways in overgrown graveyards

and I trip on weeds and reeds and more
swastikas desecrate cemetery gates.

Caretakers moved away or were murdered.
Tainted tombstones stacked fifteen deep

choke on Polish slurs. German insults.
I stumble into Auschwitz chasing the dead.

A fat gray cat with red blades for eyes
chases me. Hisses and growls. I run away

and hear an almost human-like voice
shout *RAUS RAUS RAUS*. Razor-blades

for eyes glare. I return to an unsettled
Jewish quarter where ancient goblets

filled with the honey liqueur of tears
overflow onto a Vistula River of sacrifice

and sin. Inside a modern café I devour
chocolate babka and English translations

that read, *what is poetry which does not
save Nations or people?* so I must unearth

Czesław Miłosz to ask him if the dead
are still *disguised as birds* because

while walking in Auschwitz this morning,
I saw a gray cat I suspect might be—

IN THE WARSAW GHETTO, APRIL 1941

This morning—alive—she treads narrow fetid alleyways.
    Trips on rats   roaches
        and every path she plods
        is desecrated with tattered Torah verse.
Sewage bleeds from sidewalk grates
    the way volcanos spit out
        viscous ash and lava.
She steals a view through
        needle-size cracks in a wall.
Inhales. Inhales. Inhales.
        Orange Lilies bloom on the other side.
          She tries to steal a scent of Spring.
A pungent stench
    of pork skin ripens; raids her
        fleeting fragrance of relief.
Even a sense of not smelling—
but a memory of Springtime—
    is a refuge.
Tonight
    her predictions unfold—
        old men and women
        rolled like sausages in bacon fat
        heaved and piled
    onto pavement that never asked
    to witness murder or arrange the dead.

    And on the other side of a wall—
like the silent Amidah—
        Orange Lilies bloom and bow
            while voices crack like dried-out twigs
      and gently chant the Kaddish.

PHONE CALL – MARCH 11, 2020

i just went for a long walk on the Strip   Mama says
i tell her it's freezing in Vegas today   dress warm
she answers *freezing*   not in Vegas   what's wrong
with you   you know she continues   they asked me
they asked me again   about   my presentation
with the dogs dancing on red towels   remember
i told you about it yesterday   of course i lie again
are you ready for the presentation i ask   she asks
ready for what   hmmm what dogs   time for a walk
do i sound okay   do i sound off   how do i sound

you sound great Mama   my words larger lies daily

BOSNIA UPDATE, MAY 1992
–for Sara K.

"Nobody even knows Yugoslavia is a European country
that it shares a sea with Italy!" she screams into the
phone. I don't know if it was the early hour

and I was sound asleep or San Francisco's
ubiquitous fog—thicker at 6AM—that prompted
me to suggest she brew some coffee. Toast a bagel.

Water your flowers. Instead she continues.
"Twenty-two Bosnians killed in Sarajevo. Mass graves
in Srebrenica. Slaughtered. They're being butchered!"

Eat something I plea. Drink coffee. Tea.
Anything. She ignores me so I listen half-awake
as she reads from *The New York Times*

"Serbians Attack Major Power Lines in Sarajevo.
No Electricity, Bread, or Water for Bosnians.
Suspicions Arise: Concentration Camps Again?"

"Suspicions!?! It IS genocide. Damn Muslims they say.
Nobody cares." I read a baffling piece to her.
A sidebar. Something about a musician

in Sarajevo playing cello amidst sniper fire.
For twenty-two Bosnians dead. Queuing for bread.
Killed by mortar fire. Or was it death by starvation.

She tries to cry. Drink your coffee. Eat I tell her.
"A cellist? Really?" she asks. "What did he play?"

BREAD LINE, MAY 1992

You ask me am I crazy for playing the cello,
why do you not ask if they are not crazy for shelling Sarajevo?
—Vedran Smailovic

        Every day for twenty-two days in Sarajevo
in the middle of a civil war
              a musician sits outside playing cello

while mortar shells fall outside his window.
In full view of snipers
        every day for twenty-two days in Sarajevo

he plays Albinoni's Adagio
dressed in formal concert attire.
              A musician sits outside playing cello,

howitzer shells whistle, strings plucked by his bow.
Amidst crumbling rubble in open air
        every day for twenty-two days in Sarajevo

he plays for the dead, for his city, for his sorrow
for twenty-two friends and neighbors murdered by mortar fire.
              A musician sits outside playing cello

for twenty-two lives turned into a human inferno
waiting in line for bread in the market square.
        Every day for twenty-two days in Sarajevo
              A musician sits outside playing cello.

ROSES OF SARAJEVO

    after war   craters remain
                    where lilies and orchids
              once grew
citizens   return   to   burned kitchens
torn curtains
            barren gardens
red resin fills cavernous sidewalks
      craters that look like blood stains or red roses

what side were you on?
           frequent question 25 years later

I knew your grandmother in Boston
      before 1990s   before the war
         before craters resembled
                            red roses
she rolled out layers and layers of dough
like white rose petals
    I never tasted
    baklava until her treacly pastries
    sweetened my lips
before Sarajevo shattered
    before broken roses
      before
           a bread line was target practice
           for hungry snipers

she asked me about your brother
   did he did he my grandson did he survive?

   no he snipers
   downtown Sarajevo flattened

he your grandson
     in a field of red roses
       mortars

your brother he wore your amulet
     like resin like blood stains like
          red roses

TO BE CONTINUED

On my Iranian passport, it reads
I cannot go to the Occupied Lands.
Maybe that's why Rumi wrote
The wound is the place where the light enters you.

I cannot go to the Occupied Lands
because desert light distorts the horizon and
The wound is the place where the light enters you.
I lose my way in a desert

because desert light distorts the horizon and
I dream I visit my mother in Tehran.
I lose my way in a desert.
Define history.

I dream I visit my mother in Tehran
and forgive the Guard who jailed my father.
Define history.
I share espresso and kebab with a stranger

and forgive the Guard who jailed my father.
Define peace.
I share espresso and kebab with a stranger and
we watch the sun set over the Dead Sea.

Define peace.
The distance between landmines and laughter as
we watch the sun set over the Dead Sea.
On my Iranian passport, it reads

RIVEN

I'm thinking about a room
in Budapest where I once slept

On the other side of the wall
was Agnes with her red hair

and ice skates from before
the occupation—I don't remember

any part of the room but I recall
a torrent of sunlight poured

into the kitchen every morning
over marmalade, tea, and toast

Agnes showed me her Budapest
before the war—Café Muvész

on Andrássy út where she indulged
on chocolate cakes with fresh cream,

the Opera House where she learned
about Wagner when she first saw *The Ring*—

she slowly guided me through City Park
where she skated every winter

and fell in love   she showed me
the bench they met on   flirted together

That was before hitler
before the occupation   before

her friends returned from the camps
as shadows and whispers after war

You know what I miss most she said—
skating in City Park, so I never

return in winter—too many
reminders of my first

and only love—
before he was dead

TOMBS, WHILE A CITY SLEEPS

I was sitting in mcsorley's.   outside it was New York and beautifully snowing.

—E. E. Cummings

HOLD ON, MANHATTAN, HOLD ON

Silence is strong and something is wrong
Like one of those summer nights
it's sleeping in a city skyline
after a scorching August Sunday

Like one of those summer nights
when humidity finally breaks
after a scorching August Sunday
and sun sets and everyone is too tired

when humidity finally breaks
We sit on stoops   porches   fire escapes
and sun sets and everyone is too tired
to do anything so we smash pots and pans

We sit on stoops   porches   fire escapes
Tonight feels like that kind of August Sunday
to do anything so we smash pots and pans
We practice Beethoven to pass time

Tonight feels like that kind of August Sunday
so we wait for friends to text
We practice Beethoven to pass time
Tonight we wait for friends' next breath

so we wait for friends to text
We sit   We inhale   We wait
Tonight we wait for friends' next breath
Breathe Friend Breathe

We sit   We inhale   We wait
We wonder about our next cup of coffee
Breathe Friend Breathe
We stand in warrior pose and count stars

We wonder about our next cup of coffee
It's sleeping in a city skyline
We stand in warrior pose and count stars
Silence is strong and something is wrong

BEYOND WONDERLAND

      New York rain stipples
           early evening and crabapples
at the corner of 5th Avenue and 74th.

Alice, the Mad Hatter,
and Dormouse greet protestors
    who march six feet apart, masked

        against droplets and shrapnel.

In this year,
          we inherit our
          shame.

          Beyond a fantasy
that provides shelter
for a weary decade—

beyond the Hudson River—
home to kayaks and escape routes
    beyond Museum Mile

        marbled with undulating light
          and shade for a parade of marchers—
  beyond Sheep Meadow speckled

        with pigeons and coffins
a trail of coffee cups
gives way to blood stains.

In this year,
        a meat locker

    stores our dead.

It is June.

    An almost summer sun dangles
        heavy as a grapefruit. It threatens
        to break through a round

of purple clouds and corpses. I ask my friend
    if I can move in when the end
        is near. She says the apocalypse arrived.

            We barely survived.

    In this year,
        we weep more   for the living

    than for the dead.

DAVID, WHERE ARE YOU NOW?

    a flaneur floating stardust
        with a *screwed down hairdo*
            Bowie saunters
            the Bowery and Lower East Side
        like *the Spiders from Mars*
        glittery glam jams his guitar
        like *a leper messiah*
    fearless stride   discerning smile
He whisks away
    stilted echoes
    from the other side of a wall.

    Does he feel
        a planet crashing
Bowie, if you're out there, the desperate seek your song

            We can be heroes
            For ever and ever

Earth starves for your melody   your *sound and vision*
    We want to piano cello feel
        your songs across our collarbone
           cooling calming comforting us

        We miss you
            There's a Starman waiting in the sky
            He'd like to come and meet us…

    gone   our protector of TruthNRockNRoll

        so instead we dance your daring harmonies

          we dance to forget
                        we dance for breath

Bowie, glimmering glass ghost

leading us   urging us   leaving us

                Oh man, wonder if he'll ever know
                He's in the best selling show
                Is there life on Mars?

We search our streets   our city   our country
for Ziggy   for Starman   for our Blind Prophet

                Can you hear me, Major Tom?

                Can you save us, Major Tom?

BECAUSE MY COUNTRY BROKE

I sit in an ex's backyard. Peppers and parsnips
recover from a rare April frost. We do not.

Today is May in a season of plague. Heavy
rains and fungi infect carrots and kale struggling

to grow and I brace for the next round of contagion,
uprooted trees, and bruised egos. I listen to birds

cackle and watch them eat from odd-named
bird feeders called suet and thistle. I like

the way two proud robins play and mate.
I wonder how love works, how love roots.

Years of almost. Looking backwards.
Un-learning mistakes. Recalling how my use

of chopsticks irked an ex. More at home
in crowds carrying protest signs than planting

peas and scallions with a "you" year after year.
I am more secure in history than in love.

Maybe Grandma Rose was right: "My dear shayna maidel—
wanderlust in your muscles, stardust in your soul,

rootless running forsaking partnering coupling
settling—will remain a solitary pink anemone."

I met him at a bus stop in pouring rain.
Seeking refuge from a deluge, I walked

inside his garden shop and missed my bus.
Today, I gather bleeding hearts

in his backyard and watch him harvest
dahlias and peonies for someone else.

BREATH

This once was a park
now it is a hospital—
Our mouths—infectious

Silence and distance
We rehearse a new lexis—
I attempt to sign

Earth snores and loots our
oxygen—Introduces
isolation—masked

I read loneliness
kills as much as smoking does
Soon I will be dead

SHALL WE DANCE?

A night we danced five hours
you asked if I thought you were
too tall to dance and I laughed.

A pumpkin moon lit the city
that night. Beneath a gourd
we danced some more.

Tonight, a steel crescent
looms above Manhattan.
I think about our September

waltz a hundred years
ago or was it four when
you and I were in step

when New York City was—

I miss you when I drink
coffee and read the best carrot
cake on the planet lives

in an old Bronx bakery
or a family-owned vineyard
in Salinas Sicily somehow

finds me at poet@yes.edu and emails
an invite to a futures wine tasting.
I choose to believe we never existed

at the same time. Easier than
a memory—or was it an illusion.
Suspended nights when we could

dance rooftop to rooftop. Arm
in arm beneath a Manhattan
skyline before a quarantine

when New York City was—

PHONE CALL – SEPTEMBER 23, 2020

hi Mama   hi hi how are you hi she's laughing
i ask do you know who i am   of course of course
I know you're the one who calls you're the one
who you visited yesterday we hiked the canyons
right we were in   in Red Rock   did you come
back from New Yawk   did you see your father
i know who you are   i know   how's your father
did you see canyon deer dancing on the cactus
was New Yawk fun how did i look do i look okay

i haven't seen Mama since before the pandemic
my father's been dead 12 years Mama never hiked

you look great Mama   we had fun in New Yawk

WHAT IS HOME

*To be occupied or conquered is nothing—
to remain is all!*

–Anne Sexton

WHEN THERE ARE NINE

I travel home a hundred years ago
to visit my Bubby Dora and Grandma Rose
when they were women in their

twenties, thirties, forties
with a fat future but slim options.
Henry Street Settlement

is where my Mama learned to be a girl.
Where my Mama learned from
the grit and guts of her Mother

and her Mother. I return with Mama.
When she shared her history with me
I held my breath and listened

to every detail I did not know.
Every pulse from every story
of a young girl. My Mama

who loves books, butterflies
Brooklyn Dodgers, Harry Belafonte.
Who played basketball and stickball

and loved dissecting mice and frogs
Who was taught to cook and wear
A-line dresses and balance books

on her head so she could secure
a date to high school dances.
My Mama who read the books

instead and dreamed of college
she'd never attend—until we drove
from Jersey to Boston to Burlington

in search of college for me.
My Mama's Mother,
my Grandma Rose who posed

as loyal wife and mother
baked dozens of cakes for holidays
secretly mailed me twenty-dollar bills

because I was a girl with no plans
to marry a man like her husband
my Grandpa Harry. Grandma Rose

helped me digest the NASDAQ
NYSE   S&P   our debt plus
something called volatility.

Henry Street Settlement—
where my Mama
her Mother and her Mother   learned

REVISITING BROOKLYN
—in memory of Grandma Rose

I.
Ocean Parkway's promenade with you, Grandma.
I watch you play mahjong with old friends—

6 BAM, 8 DOT, GOING DEAD—foreign
to me as Russian itself. I enter your history

and leave mine. After you win, Little Odessa Café.
I listen while you order in Yiddish and Russian—

chocolate cake with syrupy black cherries
that sweeten bitter black teas. I ask if you

think I'll ever marry. You tell me if it's bashert,
now pass the tea. I tell you, it must be bashert.

You say, you're lucky, now eat, enjoy, and order
a second chocolate cake. How am I lucky?

If you never marry, you'll never divorce.
Grandma Rose never divorced and wished

she had. For her, lucky was Grandpa Harry
dying first while she was still young enough

to see the world and eat chocolate cake
on every continent. We walk Kings Highway

arm in arm—bester freynt holding tight our
memories that taste of matzoh balls and honey cake.

II.
Our Lower East Side before I discover
Boston and you explore the world.

Lox-and-sable Sam on Rivington plies us
with extra smoked fish trim. Magda's

knitting shop on Stanton. Your brimming
bags with skeins of wool she cannot sell.

On Brighton 5th, a final nod to cake and tea.
The way you stare at me—

I return to Brooklyn decades later
to bury you. On Brighton Beach I hear

3 CRAK, 7 BAM, GOING DEAD.
In Little Odessa Café, I order

chocolate cake and syrupy black cherries
to sink into my tea. I eat. I drink. Alone.

You're lucky, I hear you say in Russian.

WE'LL BUILD AND WE'LL FIGHT
—in memory of Grandma Ida

Mornings, I visit, we sit at your kitchen table musing
over the Russian couple in 4L who devours sticks

of butter like bananas and bananas with utensils.
You stare at me—wistful. I am eight. You still dance.

These kitchen walls hold your broken dreams
in a language I do not understand. Songs we sing

in an accent I cannot understand. Woodblocks inked
in red and white from a country's borders I will not cross.

We navigate downtown Passaic—our medina
of the West. A maze of streets dotted by immigrants'

boutiques. Sparkly dresses and shiny gowns.
I want one. Your sewing suffices, you deem.

I never understand your eyes. You have no words
for this silent pain. Instead you sing songs

that sound like war to disguise your hurt—
so I cannot see. If you speak Portuguese,

the word you're looking for is Saudade.
Quickly walk past window dressing toward

Kresge's luncheon counter. Slowly slurp down
chocolate root-beer floats. Rewards for not

buying bourgeoisie, you brag. Were you loved?
Did you love? I never met your brother.

Two years later you wave goodbye. Along
the Hudson a floating castle appears

before my ten-year-old eyes. I am your home
but Minsk calls you back one last time.

Decades later I will arrange rocks on a rock—
your tombstone—but this year I wait for you.

Today, in a Passaic with too much bling,
we stand outside a drive-thru burger shop

where we once drank Kresge's ice-cream soda pop.
Bail bond kiosks hide bourgeoisie mannequins.

Bitter tales deposit in your murky eyes. Minsk
remains an anthem infused with old wounds.

Ghosts of Cossacks reappear. Come back
to flaunt today's pogroms. Did you love

your mother? Did your father love you?
Were you a poet? A translator? Did you stitch

flags or uniforms? You never explain your role
in the Revolution, so I emerge from history

with my own fight. At your funeral, I recall
battle cries for workers' rights. Songs we sang—

United, we're strong; let us march toward the dawn
                Of a brave, new workers' world.

Why did your manifesto grip you so tight?
What happened to your mother and father?

I was afraid to ask. Afraid of what you know.
Afraid of your past. Afraid of what I'd learn.

Afraid I would not understand.

MEMORY, IN FIVE PARTS

I. Desert Dance

Two hawks glide a tango low inside a red rock
canyon wall. Hypnotic flight dazzles Mama

and lightning's running through her eyes.
Wildly, her shaky hands conduct a rising

skyline symphony and two obliging hawks
encircle desert cacti scorched in unforgiving

arid wind. Mama wobbly weaves between
dry earth, lizards, hot pink sky, yet never

wonders why and forgets to ask. I hold her
shaky hands and guide her onto level ground

Slow motion, we gently waltz
with soaring hawks and desert wind

One two three. One two three.
I hold on tight. Mama smiles.

II. Leaving Las Vegas

First, her Lower East Side-Brooklyn
"trump is a bastid" accent dwindles. Next,

her familiar Passaic, New Jersey
"how ah you come faw dinnah" lexicon

muddles. Sometimes, she forgets
where she lives and tells me,

"I wawked faw miles on Broadway befaw dinnah
was served at my Plaza suite." Somewhere

between a desert dance and the Vegas Strip,
I remember Mama is my best friend

and we have many more waltzes and red rocks
to ramble. Plans to digest. Memories to eat.

Years of Mama to untangle. Loudly,
Mama is leaving Las Vegas. I silently

listen when she declares Sam the magician
on Las Vegas Boulevard asks her to marry him.

I witness
Mama smiles.

III. Visiting Normal

Some days she remembers it all and asks about
Jackie Luis Randi. She regales us with yesterdays

when she took Alison and me to see *The Fantasticks.
A Chorus Line. Search for Signs of Intelligent Life in the Universe.*

A long time ago and what feels like far away
we used to walk Delancey Street, Rivington,

Quentin, Kings Highway. My little sister, Mama, and me
eating bagels, smoked salmon, bialys. Alison and I search

for signs of intelligent life.
Mama smiles.

IV. Chance

Las Vegas wreaks havoc on Mama's memory.
Her thinning "I'm happy I'm happy

I'm happy" memory. Alison and I
navigate a family history—our inconvenient

rearview mirror forces us to "Kick Ass Take Names"
our father used to say. Into assisted living

she moves. Two hawks, red rock, a shrinking
schedule her view. We recycle our past

and shred our memories to keep pace
with Mama. We plan for nothing

but surprise because when the inevitable arrives
timing jails itself deep inside desert canyon walls.

Logic laughs.
Mama smiles.

V. Losing Her

I am losing Mama every day in different ways
and today I learn to stop seeking her advice

because when I cried to her about losing
my job and my boyfriend she wanted to drive

cross-country and move in with me. Each day
Alison and I say goodbye, Mama gifts us

with creative prose. Visits from fake rabbis
who hold galas in her honor in a land

of make-believe. Every day she makes sense
is a relief as we watch Logic kick her ass

She asks about my sons.
I have no children.

Happy, I say.
Mama smiles.

LAS VEGAS

Dusk follows me inside red rock
canyon walls. One eagle, one lizard,
    one memory call me from deep inside

a canyon. I lie down on hot chocolate
sculpted boulders and listen to a memory,
a canyon story cloaked inside a crevice

What does a red rock remember?

This is how memory unfolds
Oxygen   Time   Rain storms   Flash floods
Cranberry rock forms where Mama

once watched a hawk circle above
the canyon for an hour or did she
if she does not remember. She sits

in a wheelbarrow because I cannot
will not pair wheel
                      with chair.

Did I lock my door before leaving for Las Vegas?

I seek possibility. allsprayer kills possibility
I call alzhei–ers allsprayer because the real word
plunders. My word prays so she sits in a

wheelbarrow with allsprayer. I feel better
Does Mama? I lock my door every single
day sometimes every single three times

a day. I do not believe in prayer. Yet I pray
every single ten times a day she will stand
up sit down in a chair not a wheelbarrow

Why did we eat Chinese food every Christmas Day?

I pray she confuses my sister and me
because she is tired not because she has
allsprayer. I pray she asks to meet Alison and me

to eat shrimp dumplings with her at Hop Kee
on Canal Street at midnight. I pray she embarrasses
me and flirts with the owners and their sons

What is the color of memory?

I pray she teaches me once more
how to fold a fitted sheet so all four
corners neatly match. I pray allsprayer

is alls a mistake. Memory is the color
of red rock deep inside a canyon
where Mama unknowingly slides

CANYON BALLAD

What if I lose my words
        Mama's losing hers
        inside her self-contained desert
        she hears cacti cry

She climbs red rock
        white rock   hunts deer
        she inhabits webs
        beyond assisted living

Mama   do you remember when
        wrong verb
        am I losing my words
        how do I ask what do you recall

They tell us she needs memory care
        how will they care for her memory
        they forgot to tell us how to speak
        with her   to her   about her

Through her   without her   watch her
        don't speak   sing
        she knows   I know she knows
        words disappear   she knows

Am I okay she asks today
        yes Mama
        will you tell me when I am not okay she asks
        yes Mama

I started lying to her years ago
    you will be okay Mama
    this is like a cold
    she was a social butterfly

She loved butterflies
    I write in past tense
    as if she is dead   isn't she
    my Mama

Who did not understand silence
    I used to ask her   no   I used to tell her
    Mama please take a breath
    for a few   if I only knew

Did you write a happy poem yet
    Mama asks
    yes I lie and make one up now
    for you Mama

Somewhere deep inside red rock canyon
    eagles soar   butterflies glow
    cacti dance   songs reside   deer dreams survive
    Mama's words   Mama's breath   Mama's love

        to memory care she moves

HEAT

I don't know where to go. I drive south on the Garden State Parkway. I listen to Carole King—*Stayed in bed all mornin' just to pass the time...*I sing out of tune.

Wind slaps my face. Burns my wet eyes. I scream more than sing. I sing for my dead father. I sing for my Mama's loofah brain. I sing for loss. For love. *It's too late, baby, now...*

I drive crosstown to a Christmas party. I notice a tall man in blue tennis sweats. Baseball mitts for hands. Scruffy handsome. I wear a thin black cocktail dress. I notice him notice me. It starts to snow. I hold an empty glass of red wine. He stares.

I gape at his hands. Snow falls fast. Why are you leaving? It is the tall man. I'm afraid to drive in snow. Don't be afraid, he says. Snow is kind.

She meets the tall man for lunch. He's sitting inside. A bottle of unopened red on the table. She's nervous. His hands grope the wine cork. Eyes bluer than she recalls. Brown-gray hair. He remembers I drink red. He pours. She loves his hands.

He plays tennis and sings opera. She hates tennis and opera. She writes poetry and eats with chopsticks. He reads mysteries and thinks chopsticks are an affect. He walks her home. A hug.

On her coat, later that night, she notices large handprints. Do you like poetry, she wanted to ask. I don't know where to go. I still drive south on the Parkway. Starts to snow. I call Mama this morning. Did I meet dad for coffee she asks. I'm afraid to drive in snow. Is he joining you in Vegas she asks. Yes, I answer.

I exit the Parkway. My father died ten years ago. I head to the ocean. Snow is kind. No. Ocean is kind. *I feel like a fool...* I walk barefoot. Ocean is cold.

We are sitting on a mint-green couch in his living room. Flames wheeze in the fireplace. Why did you sleep downstairs last night he asks. A waning fire the only light. Hands tracing her collarbone. What's wrong, tell me.

Ask about my poems, she wants to say. He adds logs to a dying fire. He holds her. She's crying. Notice me. Like the first night. Like in Maine. Like. Like. Care. *But we just can't stay together...*

I don't know where to go. I crisscross switchbacks in Red Rock Canyon. It is 105 degrees at 10AM in October. Locals say dry heat isn't hot. They're wrong. Hot is all they know. Vegas heat is wrong.

Mama hated summer in New York. Loves it in Vegas. She tells me dry heat isn't hot it's healing. Vegas creeps beneath her skin. Did you see your father today?

I notice Mama's loofah brain holds less this time. I pull off the road and park my rental. Throw my half-naked body onto a warm red rock.

She asks about the tall man. Do you miss him. *Somethin' inside has died...*Mama's memory plays hide-n-seek but him she remembers. Snow is kind. No. Red rock is kind.

FUNERAL

wet
red
leaves
rusty
Dunlop
racquets
mourners
toss
yellow
tennis balls
and rocks
at head-
stones
Satie's
*Gymnopédie
No. 3*
inks
a single
black
rose
drops
sideways
i pivot into

mourners
Kaddish
and hear
his will-
full-ness
(always
miss a train
for one
last kiss
he said
read
read poems)
i watch
my father
and his
Dunlop
drop
into
muddy
brown
earth
wet
red

THE PUGILIST'S DAUGHTER

Because I never married
I want to marry
so I wait for a unicorn
because I am a mermaid

I am not sure what this means
because I have never seen a unicorn
or mermaid except in coloring books   films
and the Coney Island Mermaid Parade

After my last breakup
loneliness detonated its shrapnel
through my eyes   my lips   sometimes heart
Trapped   Abject   Tears clogged ducts

My last ex did not read my poems
He loved me but did not like me
He did not believe in unicorns and mermaids
and I always rode carousels alone

Because my father knew me
but did not know how
to love me   he understood me
I believed this only after he died

Because I started watching films
he suggested when he was alive—
My Brilliant Career   Intermezzo
Brief Encounter   Cool Hand Luke

My father knew my fragments
He knew I loved
the Coney Island carousel
and gave me random poems to read

Sexton   Yeats   Dickinson   Keats
I thought they were random
When I read them today
Nothing random

My father loved
the Coney Island Cyclone
He knew I was afraid so instead we rode
the carousel together

The poems my father
gave me were about love
sometimes marriage
sometimes carousels

PHONE CALL – NOVEMBER 29, 2020

what's new she asks   America has a new president
i say   hmm   oh yeah   what's that like   well he's
a grownup i say   laughing she says   they never are
Mama says   before i go to bed   this usually happens
i must tell you   blablabla   i forget   when i call you
my phone calls are before i   go to bed   when i'm
tired i   forget   what i want to say   are you writing

Mama hasn't called in five years since her diagnosis

she says i'm tired now   i love you   keep doing
whatever you're doing   don't stop   till you get
somewhere   write your poems   okay   write   write
your book   don't stop till you get somewhere
goodbye   i know   i know   i'm repeating   i know
i love you   write poems   write for me   keep writing
do i sound okay to you   i love you so much   do i
sound happy   do i   i wrote you a poem yesterday

i want to share a lifetime of stories with her from
the past five years   i want to tell her today's my
birthday but she'll cry because she can't remember
birthdays anymore   for a second she'll know

i miss you   i love you Mama   you sound happy

NOTES

Opening quote [And dreams are faces with large eyes and weak chins and broad brows that get smashed by the fists of square faces.]: From Jean Toomer's *Cane*, a collection of poetry and prose.

[Oh, but to be a boxer not a poet,] is an excerpt from Wisława Szymborska's poem, "Poetry Reading."

"The Pugilist in Twelve Rounds," [To love my father is to love his wounds.]: Cathy Linh Che's "Go Forget Your Father."

[Loneliness is solitude with a problem.]: Maggie Nelson's *Bluets*.

In "Trains Are a Failed Romance," [like dolphins can swim] is a lyric from "Heroes" by David Bowie.

In "After the One That Broke Me," [There's a Starman waiting in the sky] is a lyric in David Bowie's "Starman." [Then we should find some artificial inoculation against love, as with smallpox] is from Leo Tolstoy's *Anna Karenina*.

"Carrot Cake at the Altar" is in memory of Kristine Ann Zelazik (1963–1992), my partner in fun, whose life ended much too soon. In 1985, traveling in a divided Berlin, we did get lost and scorned in German by soldiers on the eastern side of the Wall.

[I cannot remember a time when I did not love Budapest. And today, I'm just looking for memories.]: Agnes A. is a dear friend and Holocaust survivor. In 1998, we visited Budapest together and retraced her journey.

Italicized lines in "Kraków Square" are excerpts from Czesław Miłosz's "Return to Kraków 1880."

The title, "Hollow (While Thinking About Primo Levi)" and the *not-so-famous suicide* line refer to Levi's suicide in Turin, Italy, on April 11, 1987.

I started writing "Nocturne" in 1996, while living in Kraków, to research Bennie's life before and during the war. We regularly visited Auschwitz-Birkenau. Frederic Chopin (1810–1849) was a Polish composer during the Romantic period.

In "Is That Himmler Biting His Hind Paw," italicized lines are excerpts from Czesław Miłosz's "Dedication."

"Bosnia Update, May 1992" is for my dear friend, Sara K., who taught me about the history and beauty of her country, former Yugoslavia.

"Bread Line" is inspired by the courage of cellist Vedran Smailovic, a former member of the Sarajevo Philharmonic Orchestra. The events in the poem happened, and are based on one of many tragic days in May 1992 during the siege of Sarajevo, which lasted almost four years.

In "To Be Continued," [The wound is the place where light enters you] is a quote by Rumi.

[I was sitting in mcsorley's. / outside it was New York and beautifully snowing.]: The first line from an E. E. Cummings poem.

In "David, Where Are You Now?" italicized lines are David Bowie lyrics from: "Ziggy Stardust," "Heroes," "Starman," "Life on Mars," and "Space Oddity."

[To be occupied or conquered is nothing—to remain is all!]: From "Walking in Paris," by Anne Sexton.

"When There Are Nine" is from a quote by Justice Ruth Bader Ginsburg: [When I'm sometimes asked 'When will there be enough [women on the Supreme Court]?' and I say 'When there are nine,' people are shocked.]

In "We'll Build and We'll Fight," the title and italicized lines are lyrics from the International Ladies' Garment Workers' Union (ILGWU) theme song.

Italicized lines in "Heat" are lyrics from "It's Too Late," by Carole King.

The "Phone Call" poems are real phone conversations with my mother (Mama) after her 2017 diagnosis. During 2020—the first year of the pandemic—we spoke every day for almost an hour. She was the one person in my life who had no awareness of how sad and scared I felt. With her, I had to pretend, so for one hour every day, she made me laugh. Despite her cognitive loss, she is alert, funny, and always a source of love and inspiration.

Mama still lives in Las Vegas, and our phone calls continue.

ACKNOWLEDGEMENTS

With love and gratitude, to all of my friends and family who have encouraged me from the start to keep writing poems. Thank you, always, for your ongoing support.

Rebecca Bonham, of Blue Jade Press, helped turn my manuscript into a book. Thank you for your generous spirit.

Todd Windley designed the cover art. I am grateful for your artistic vision, patience, and friendship. Thank you.

"To Be Continued" was awarded Honorable Mention in the Tom Howard/Margaret Reid Poetry Contest 2020. With gratitude to Adam Cohen, President of Winning Writers.

My Mama was a dreamer who loved to read and write poetry. She cannot read or write anymore, but when I recite my poems during our phone calls, I feel her smile all the way from Las Vegas.

This book is dedicated to Mama, with love.

Photo Credit: Luis Vieira

ABOUT THE AUTHOR

Judith Lynn Antelman is a poet and writer from Passaic, New Jersey. Her passion for travel took her to cities as far away from home as San Francisco and Krakow. When not writing or traveling, Judith plays piano, and wishes she had been a classical pianist. She holds an MFA in Creative Writing from The New School. *The Pugilist's Daughter* is her first collection of poems. Judith lives in Montclair, New Jersey.

www.ingramcontent.com/pod-product-compliance
Lightning Source LLC
Chambersburg PA
CBHW022114090426
42743CB00008B/844